DYNAMIC DUOS OF SCIENCE

ALBERT EINSTEIN
AND
SIR ARTHUR EDDINGTON

Gareth Stevens
PUBLISHING

Mary Colson

Please visit our website, **www.garethstevens.com**. For a free color catalog of all our high-quality books, call toll free 1-800-542-2595 or fax 1-877-542-2596.

Library of Congress Cataloging-in-Publication Data

Colson, Mary.
Albert Einstein and Sir Arthur Eddington / by Mary Colson.
p. cm. -- (Dynamic duos of science)
Includes index.
ISBN 978-1-4824-1293-2 (pbk.)
ISBN 978-1-4824-1276-5 (6-pack)
ISBN 978-1-4824-1470-7 (library binding)
1. Einstein, Albert, -- 1879-1955 -- Juvenile literature. 2. Eddington, Arthur Stanley, Sir, 1882-1944. 3. Physicists -- Biography -- Juvenile literature. I. Colson, Mary. II. Title.
QC16.E5 C65 2015
530--d23

First Edition

Published in 2015 by
Gareth Stevens Publishing
111 East 14th Street, Suite 349
New York, NY 10003

© Gareth Stevens Publishing

Produced by: Calcium, www.calciumcreative.co.uk
Designed by: Keith Williams
Edited by: Sarah Eason and Jennifer Sanderson
Picture research by: Rachel Blount

Photo credits: Cover: Library of Congress: George Grantham Bain Collection (right), Harris & Ewing Collection (left); Shutterstock: Vadim Sadovski (background); Inside: California Institute of Technology: Richard Massey/ Durham University 28; CERN: 42, Laurent Guiraud 43; Dreamstime: Julija Sapic 22; Library of Congress: 21, George Grantham Bain Collection 5t, 37b, NYWT&S 36, Press Illustrating Service 35, F. Foxton, Scarborough 20; NASA: 7, A. Fruchter/ERO Team/STScI 33, Goddard Space Flight Center 5b, Jet Propulsion Laboratory 24; Shutterstock: Arindambanerjee 41, Catwalker 45, Jules2000 38r, Hayati Kayhan 14, Koya979 1, 6, Krasowit 15, MilanB 17, Mironov 44, Vadim Sadovski 3, 16, Lev Savitskiy 11, Vasilieva Tatiana 9, Anatolii Vasilev 31, Vladimir Wrangel 29, YANGCHAO 32; University of Cambridge, Institute of Astronomy Library: Warwick Brookes 18; Wikimedia Commons: 19, Bcrowell 13, Lucien Chavan 10, Benjamin Couprie, Institut International de Physique de Solvay 40, Paul Ehrenfest 38l, Alfred Hutter 37t, Brocken Inaglory 23, Steve Jurvetson 12, Charles Levy 39, Library of Congress 26, Life Magazine 30, Georg Pahl 27, Sage Ross 25, Charles Russell 34, Ferdinand Schmutzer 4, The authorities of the Canton of Aargau, Switzerland 8.

Printed in the United States of America

CPSIA compliance information: Batch #CS15GS: For further information contact Gareth Stevens, New York, New York at 1-800-542-2595.

Contents

CHAPTER 1

A Very Big Bang!

Most people know the name Albert Einstein. The scientist with the wild, crazy hair and twinkling eyes changed our understanding of the universe forever.

Einstein explained how gravity works, discovered what black holes in space are, predicted that atoms contain energy, and turned previous scientific theories about space, time, and the universe on their heads.

Albert Einstein changed how we see the universe.

IN THEIR OWN WORDS

Albert Einstein said:

"I think and think for months and years. Ninety-nine times, the conclusion is false. The hundredth time I am right ..."

Eddington: The Hidden Talent

Much less famous today is the English scientist Sir Arthur Eddington. However, Eddington is crucial to the story of this dynamic duo. Eddington was an astrophysicist and without him Einstein's theories might never have been brought to the attention of the scientific world and might never have been proven.

Eddington was more famous than Einstein at the time, but it was Einstein and his revolutionary ideas that caused the biggest bang. Eddington proved, promoted, and explained Einstein's complex theories to the wider world. The story of these scientists is one of the rock star of physics and the quiet man of science.

Arthur Eddington was the most brilliant astrophysicist of his day.

Einstein and Eddington studied and explained the wonders of space.

What Is Gravity?

What keeps us from floating off into space, and why does something that you drop fall to the ground? These were questions that puzzled Einstein, so he set out to find the answers.

Gravity attracts all objects toward each other. It keeps the planets in orbit around the stars, just like Earth orbits the sun. Earth's gravity is what keeps objects from drifting into space. Gravity is also what causes things to drop to the ground and the reason that there are tides in the oceans. It also helps make the wind blow.

Gravity is an essential force. Earth's gravity holds us down on the ground.

Understanding how gravity works means that humans can explore space.

Newton and Einstein

The great English scientist Sir Isaac Newton calculated and predicted all the forces at work in the universe. Until Einstein came along, Newton's theories had been accepted as fact for more than 200 years. Einstein showed that gravity is the effect of objects, such as the sun and planets, on space. He proved that big objects push or bend the space around them.

BEHIND THE SCIENCE

A famous story tells how Newton discovered his ideas about gravity from watching an apple fall from a tree in his orchard. Newton believed that the same force—gravity—controlled the apple and the moon. He believed that gravity was a force between two objects that pulled them together.

Childhood, Faith, and Science

Albert Einstein excelled at math and physics, but he found school difficult and struggled in many subjects. Arthur Eddington, on the other hand, did very well at school and won a scholarship to study at Trinity College, the University of Cambridge, in England.

The Young Einstein

Albert Einstein was born in Ulm, Germany, on March 14, 1879. His family moved from Germany to Italy because of his father's work. When he was 17, Einstein passed his exams and went to study at the Institute of Technology in Zurich, Switzerland. In 1905, he received his doctorate from the University of Zurich. Einstein's family was Jewish, and later in life when he visited Israel, he was invited to become its president.

Even Einstein was not brilliant at every subject, as his school report (opposite) shows!

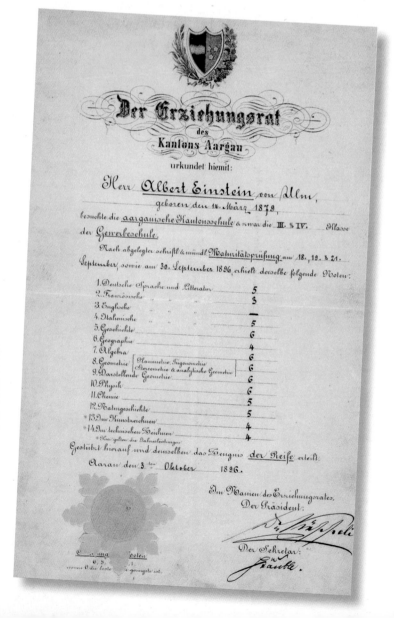

Eddington studied at the University of Cambridge, England.

The Young Eddington

Arthur Eddington was born on December 28, 1882. His family were Quakers who did not believe in war. His father was a highly educated man who died of typhoid when Eddington was just four years old. Eddington was very close to his sister, Winifred. She helped him to keep his Quaker faith when the horrors of World War I made him question it. Like Einstein, Eddington was fascinated by math. He won every math prize at school and went on to win others at the university in Cambridge.

IN THEIR OWN WORDS

Einstein said:

"I am neither very clever nor especially gifted. I am only very, very curious."

9

The Odd Couple

At the turn of the twentieth century, Einstein and Eddington were leading very different academic lives. Eddington was a scientific superstar: he was one of the youngest professors at the University of Cambridge and making his mark in the world of astrophysics. Einstein was struggling to find a teaching position in a university physics department.

Einstein was married with a young child and so he took a job in the patent office in Bern, Switzerland, to support his family. His job was to evaluate applications for scientific inventions. During his time at the patent office, Einstein was still working on his theories, conducting experiments, and thinking about the universe.

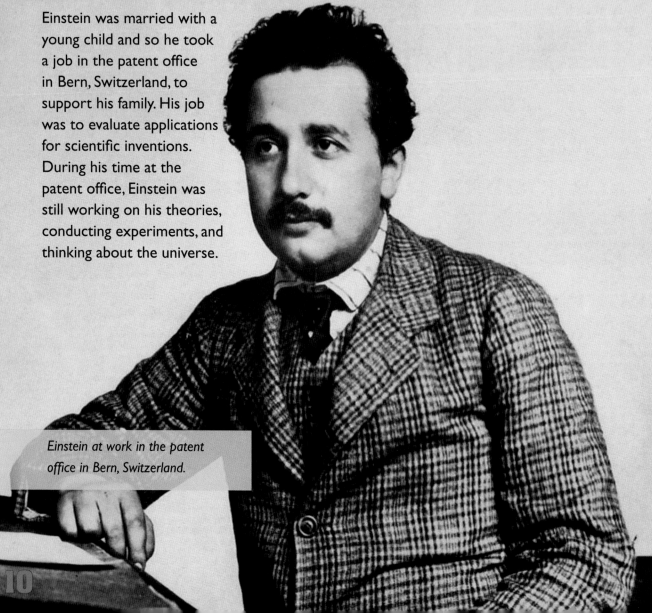

Einstein at work in the patent office in Bern, Switzerland.

The universe is made up of thousands of different galaxies such as this one.

The Big Bang Theory

Today, many scientists believe that the universe was created more than 13 billion years ago after a gigantic explosion called the Big Bang. The theory states that before the explosion all the matter in the universe was concentrated into a tiny spot. The heat of the explosion caused the universe to expand. Afterward, gravity pulled tiny particles, called atoms, together to make the stars and planets. Albert Einstein wrestled with these complex ideas to the point that even he found them confusing.

IN THEIR OWN WORDS

Einstein was so puzzled by the Big Bang that he said:

"I must confess that . . . I was visited by all sorts of nervous conflicts . . . I used to go away for weeks in a state of confusion."

11

CHAPTER 2

1905: The Year the Universe Changed

In 1905, Einstein published four scientific papers that sent shockwaves through the world of science. In them he explained the universe and how it works in terms of space, time, mass, and energy. The ideas and theories in the 1905 papers have shaped modern physics.

One of the papers explained how to measure the size of molecules in a liquid and another explored how to figure out the movement of the molecules. In the third paper, Einstein described how light comes in chunks called photons, while the last paper introduced his master idea: the Special Theory of Relativity.

Einstein's revolutionary theories about the universe changed the views of the scientists of his era and continue to influence scientists of today.

Einstein often met up with his friends, the philosopher Konrad Habicht and the mathematician Maurice Solovine, to discuss science, philosophy, and literature.

Time and Space

Newton believed that time and space were separate and fixed. Einstein said that they connect to form space-time. This means that time, length, and mass will have different measurements depending on the position and speed of movement of the person making the measurement. If you could see a rocket move through space at almost the speed of light, it would look shorter than it is and its clocks would move more slowly. Additionally, the rocket's mass would increase with speed.

BEHIND THE SCIENCE

The theories in Einstein's papers put him in direct conflict with Newton. Many scientists could not believe that Einstein was right or that he had the nerve to question the great Newton.

What Is E=mc²?

Einstein's Special Theory of Relativity described the behavior of objects at high speeds. It also contained the famous equation E=mc²—what do these letters, symbols, and numbers mean?

In Einstein's equation, E stands for energy, m is mass, and c is the speed of light. Einstein calculated that there was a relationship between the energy and the mass of an object. The equation says that the amount of energy held within a piece of matter is the same as its mass times the speed of light squared. This means that the mass of an object can be converted into energy. Even a tiny object such as an atom can release a huge amount of energy in a chain reaction.

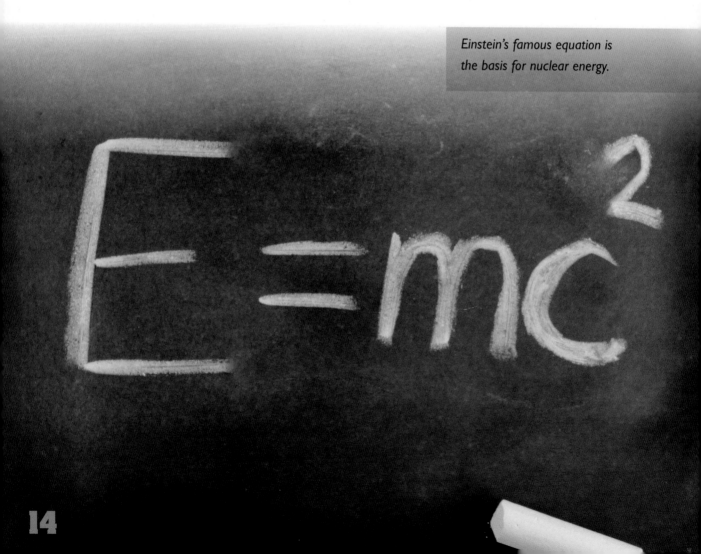

Einstein's famous equation is the basis for nuclear energy.

When a nuclear explosion occurs, the atoms continue to split until all the energy of the explosion is used up.

Splitting an Atom

In 1917, the New Zealander Ernest Rutherford was the first person to split an atom. When an atom's nucleus splits, it releases neutrons that bump into other atoms, splitting them and releasing more neutrons. Nuclei continue to split. The chain reaction releases a huge amount of energy. When radioactive uranium atoms are split, the explosive chain reaction makes nuclear power. If this chain reaction isn't controlled, a nuclear explosion occurs and radioactive particles pollute the air. This is harmful to both human health and the environment.

BEHIND THE SCIENCE

By the 1930s, scientists were using Einstein's equation to make nuclear bombs. As a lifelong pacifist, Einstein was horrified and spent much of his later years campaigning for peace.

Bending Light and Expanding Space

Einstein's work on light and space went farther than any scientist had ever gone before. In fact, he explained that the universe was not a fixed space. Instead, it expanded.

Einstein's mathematical equations suggested that the universe must be expanding or becoming smaller, but it could not be standing still. Einstein figured out that any object with a large mass (such as a star or a planet) pushes on space and bends it. This was the opposite of Newton's theories and so surprising that Einstein thought he must have made a mistake in his calculations.

Both Einstein and Eddington were fascinated by space, light, and stars.

Passing a beam of light through a prism displays the color spectrum of light.

BEHIND THE SCIENCE

Newton proposed the theory that light is made up of tiny particles. Other physicists, such as Christian Huygens, said that light moved as a wave. By the early twentieth century, Max Planck suggested that light was made up of quanta—small packets of energy.

The Problem with Light

Understanding the behavior of light is very important to physicists. Light is part of the electromagnetic spectrum. The electromagnetic spectrum includes all visible light as well as invisible light, such as radio waves and X-rays. When he was 16, Einstein imagined what would happen if he chased a beam of light. Years later, this led him to understand how light moves. In 1905, he proposed that light bends, and it moves in chunks called photons as well as in waves.

Cambridge and Berlin

In the years leading up to World War I, both Einstein and Eddington continued their work. Eddington was enjoying a brilliant scientific career that saw him investigate the insides of stars.

In January 1906, Eddington went to work at the Royal Greenwich Observatory in London, England. His work on stars and planets won him a Fellowship to Trinity College, the University of Cambridge. There, his work on space, light, and the diameters of stars continued. Seven years later, he became the youngest person to become Plumian Professor of Astronomy and Experimental Philosophy. He was also made director of the Cambridge Observatory.

This photograph shows Eddington at Cambridge. He is pictured in the photograph below, in the red circle.

18

Here is Einstein in Berlin, Germany, with some of his colleagues, including his friend Max Planck (on Einstein's left).

A Rare Genius

After his 1905 papers, the scientific community was starting to catch up with Einstein. More scientists understood his theories, and his work was fast becoming recognized as very important. In 1909, Einstein became Associate Professor of Theoretical Physics at Zurich and Professor of Theoretical Physics at the German University in Prague, Czechoslovakia (now the Czech Republic) in 1911. In 1914, he became director of the Kaiser Wilhelm Institute for Physics in Berlin, thanks to his friend Max Planck. In the same year, Einstein became a German citizen.

IN THEIR OWN WORDS

Eddington said:

"I think that ... ultimately we shall find that there are many galaxies of a size equal to and surpassing our own."

CHAPTER 3
The World at War

In 1914, war broke out in Europe. During World War I, Great Britain and Germany fought on opposite sides.

In 1916, the British government introduced conscription. This meant that if you were a single man between the ages of 18 and 41 and fit, you had to join the army. Scientists at the University of Cambridge and the University of Oxford argued that the best brains of a generation should not be sent to die in the trenches. Eventually, the government agreed, and Eddington and other key scientists were allowed to continue their work. The war created a very strong anti-German feeling in Great Britain. In universities, work by German scientists was shunned. If Einstein's new theory was to reach the wider world of physicists, it was going to have to travel across enemy lines.

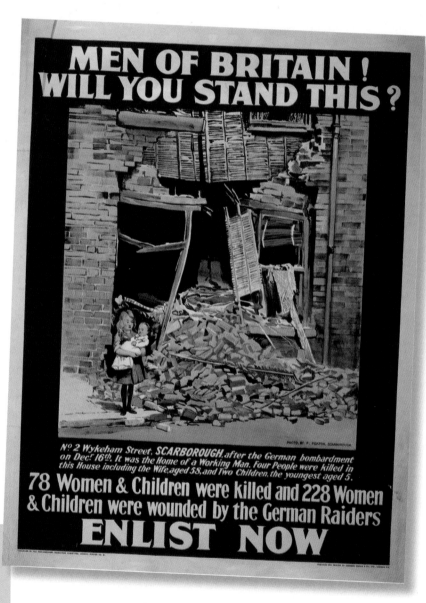

MEN OF BRITAIN! WILL YOU STAND THIS?

No 2 Wykeham Street, SCARBOROUGH, after the German bombardment on Dec! 16th. It was the Home of a Working Man. Four People were killed in this House including the Wife, aged 58, and Two Children, the youngest aged 5.

78 Women & Children were killed and 228 Women & Children were wounded by the German Raiders

ENLIST NOW

During World War I, the British government encouraged young men to join up and fight. Eddington argued against professors and scientists going to war.

The horror of the trenches of World War I made both Einstein and Eddington even more certain that war was wrong.

Posting Papers Across Enemy Lines

Between 1905 and 1916, Einstein continued working on his ideas about the universe. He wanted to understand more about time, space, light, and gravity. Einstein sent copies of his new, more developed theory to Willem de Sitter in the Netherlands. De Sitter was astounded and decided that Eddington had to read the papers, too. He thought that Eddington was the only scientist in the world with the status, intellect, and influence to understand and test Einstein's theory. Eddington could hardly believe his eyes: Einstein's theory was remarkable.

IN THEIR OWN WORDS

On the war, Einstein said:

"My pacifism is an instinctive feeling, a feeling that possesses me because the murder of men is abhorrent. My attitude is ... based on my deepest antipathy to every kind of cruelty and hatred."

21

Einstein's General Theory of Relativity

Eddington read Einstein's new theory in amazement. Einstein called it his General Theory of Relativity, and it showed he had developed his earlier ideas. In 1916, the British Astronomical Society, of which Eddington was a member, published Einstein's General Theory of Relativity.

Just like his previous great theories, the General Theory of Relativity turned the scientific community upside down and divided opinion. Many remained loyal to Newton's ideas, but Eddington thought that Einstein could be right.

Physics formulas are very complicated. The brilliant physicist Eddington became an expert in Einstein's new ideas and formulas.

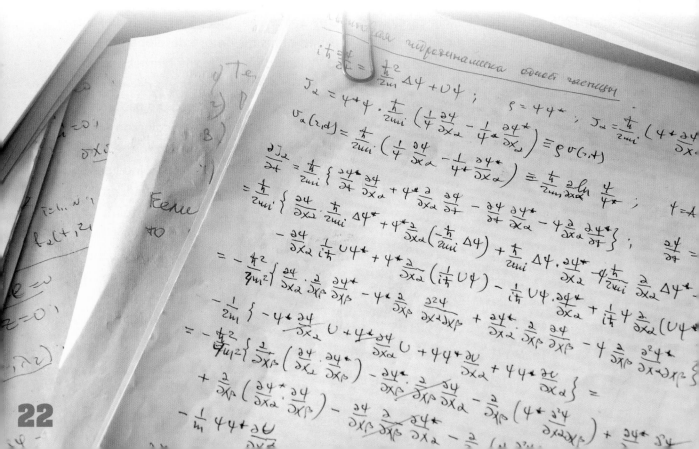

Mercury is the smallest planet in our solar system and the planet nearest the sun.

A Breakthrough

Einstein's theory shows that Mercury's orbital path around the sun changes a little each time because of gravity, so it does not just repeat the same route. Unluckily for Newton, when making calculations to do with the vastness of space, to be even a little bit wrong is to be very wrong.

BEHIND THE SCIENCE

Johannes Kepler was a German mathematician and astronomer. He studied how planets move in their orbits around stars, just like Earth orbits the sun. Newton proved Kepler's theory. He expanded upon it and believed that planets moved in straight lines in an almost egg-shaped orbit around their star. However, Newton's calculations did not accurately predict the orbit of Mercury, the planet closest to the sun. Mercury's orbit was predicted accurately only once Einstein's new theory about how gravity worked was understood.

A Friendship Through Letters

In 1916, Einstein and Eddington began writing letters to each other. They carried on doing this for the rest of their lives. Their friendship developed through a mutual respect and shared fascination with the universe—it was a meeting of minds and of shared values.

In their letters, the two scientists shared scientific thoughts and theories, and they commented on each other's work. Their discussions were highly academic. Initially, the letters were about Einstein's amazing new theory. Eddington was particularly interested in the idea that light bends in the gravitational field of the sun.

Our solar system has eight planets. Earth is the only one able to support life.

Scientists such as Einstein often used scale models of the solar system.

Great Minds Think Alike

Einstein wrote to Eddington in German, but a lot of the letters were made up of mathematical equations and formulas. Eddington understood German but, most importantly, he could also follow the math. As he studied Einstein's theory, Eddington himself became an expert in the math and physics. This was extremely useful later as he tried to persuade others that the work of a German should be taken seriously.

IN THEIR OWN WORDS

In 1919, Eddington was asked whether it was true that only three people in the world understood the General Theory of Relativity. Eddington is said to have replied:

"Who's the third?"

Public Opinion

Eddington's biggest challenge was not understanding the math of Einstein's theory but persuading others that the work of a German scientist should be looked at seriously. Some older scientists had lost sons in the war, and many others could not forgive Germany for the bloodshed.

However, the resistance toward Einstein and his work was not just based on his nationality. Einstein's claim that the great Newton had been wrong was just as much a problem for many people in the scientific world.

Eddington became Einstein's champion in English academic circles and promoted his work. Over time, Eddington convinced the scientists at the University of Cambridge and at the Royal Society that their prejudice against Einstein was unfounded.

Anti-German feeling ran high in Britain even after the war. Eddington had to work hard to convince British scholars to listen to Einstein's theories.

BRITISH EMPIRE UNION
ONCE A GERMAN — ALWAYS A GERMAN!

1914 TO 1918.

EDITH CAVELL

NEVER AGAIN!

BERLIN

REMEMBER!
Every German employed means a British Worker idle.
Every German article sold means a British article unsold.
BRITISH EMPIRE UNION: 346 STRAND, LONDON, W.C.2

Freedom of speech was banned in Germany in the 1930s, and many books written by Jewish authors, such as Einstein, were burned.

Translating Einstein

Eddington was the first person to explain the theory of relativity in the English language in a way that everyone could understand. By doing this, he helped to popularize Einstein's theory and enabled it to reach a very wide audience. In 1923, he wrote *The Mathematical Theory of Relativity*, which explained Einstein's theory. Einstein himself considered it the finest explanation of relativity in any language, even his own.

IN THEIR OWN WORDS

Einstein said:

"Equations are more important to me, because politics is for the present, but an equation is something for eternity."

CHAPTER 4

Worldwide Fame

Throughout World War I, Eddington promoted Einstein's theories and tried to encourage the scientific world to listen. However, it was his expedition to the island of Príncipe off the west coast of Africa that had the biggest impact on Einstein's place in history.

While on the island of Príncipe, Eddington tested Einstein's theory during a solar eclipse. During a total eclipse, when the moon sits in front of the sun, you can see stars that you cannot normally see because the sun is too bright. If Einstein's theory about gravity was correct, the stars with light rays that passed near the sun would appear to have been slightly shifted because their light had been curved toward the sun's gravitational field.

Today, on the island of Príncipe, a plaque celebrates Einstein's theory and Eddington's proof.

O eclipse de Sundy

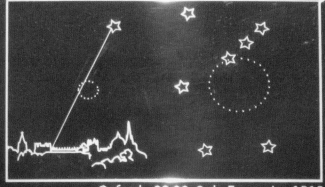

Oxford - 23:00, 9 de Fevereiro 1919

Sundy - 14:17, 29 de Maio 1919

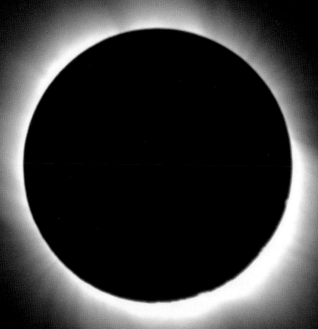

A total solar eclipse is a dramatic sight in which most of the sun's light is blocked.

A solar eclipse occurs when the moon passes directly in front of the sun and blocks most of its light from Earth.

Proving the Theory

The photographs Eddington took during the solar eclipse showed that the stars around the eclipsed sun had been moved into a slightly different position. Einstein was right—light did bend. His theory about gravity had been proven true!

Reaction to the Proof

After Eddington's proof, worldwide fame beckoned for Einstein. His ideas captured the public's imagination as well as the curiosity of scientists. Einstein became the most famous scientist on the planet, perhaps of all time. Einstein was invited on lecture tours overseas, received many honors, met kings and queens, and was treated like a star wherever he went.

Between 1921 and 1923, Einstein traveled to many countries including the United States, Great Britain, France, and Japan, as well as to the Middle East. In Britain, Einstein and Eddington finally met, and their friendship was cemented. Einstein also began commenting on political issues and promoting his pacifist beliefs. After four years of war, many people welcomed the peaceful message of the gentle genius.

Einstein is shown in an open-top car touring New York City. The brilliant scientist was given a rock star's welcome when he arrived in the city.

Today, we can see deep into space by using gravitational lenses.

Shockwaves!

Eddington's proof of Einstein's theory sent shockwaves through the scientific community, and its impact is still being felt today. The proof that light bent was used to figure out the nature of gravity. At the time, even Einstein thought that it had no further uses. However, modern physicists have applied the theory to help them find out more about deep space. Today, gravitational lenses are used to find out more about space.

BEHIND THE SCIENCE

Gravitational lenses work in a similar way to ordinary glass lenses in that they magnify light. The difference is that gravitational lenses do it on a huge scale. They enable astronomers to see objects that are otherwise too far away for even the largest telescopes on Earth.

Glittering Prizes

After more than a decade of being nominated and despite the anti-Semitic feelings toward him in Germany, Albert Einstein won the Nobel Prize in Physics in 1921. He was awarded the prize for his work on the photoelectric effect, which was a continuation of his great work on light and energy.

While Einstein was becoming the world's most celebrated scientist, Eddington was making waves of his own. During and after World War I, he carried on with his work on the interior of stars. He accepted that stars were balls of gas, but he calculated the radiation pressure needed to stop them from collapsing in on themselves. He also estimated the temperature inside stars, and by the mid-1920s, Eddington was one of the most important astrophysicists of the age.

Albert Einstein won the Nobel Prize in Physics and became the world's most famous scientist.

1921 Nobel Physics Prize 1921

Albert Einstein (G)

Grenada $1

Lasting Influence

Eddington published two works that became essential reading for all young scientists: *The Internal Constitution of the Stars* in 1926 and *The Expanding Universe* in 1933. He was made a Fellow of the Royal Society and received many other honors from scientific institutions around the world.

When stars eventually burn themselves out, they die. This takes place over many millions of years.

BEHIND THE SCIENCE

All matter on Earth is made up of atoms. Around each atom are tiny particles, called electrons, which have a negative charge. The photoelectric effect refers to the flow of electric current in a material when the material is exposed to light. The electrons break free if they get enough energy from the photons.

CHAPTER 5

Dangerous Times

By the late 1920s, Einstein had started to attract the wrong kind of attention. As a Jew, he was targeted by Hitler and the Nazis and became the target of hateful propaganda. There was even a price on the head of the world's greatest scientist.

The times were changing, and Germany was becoming a very dangerous place for anyone whom the Nazi Party viewed with suspicion. Attacks on Jewish intellectuals were becoming common. Authors, philosophers, and scientists had their books burned, and some were sent to prison. Einstein watched the events unfold with horror and began to wonder whether pacifism would work when faced with such a powerful enemy.

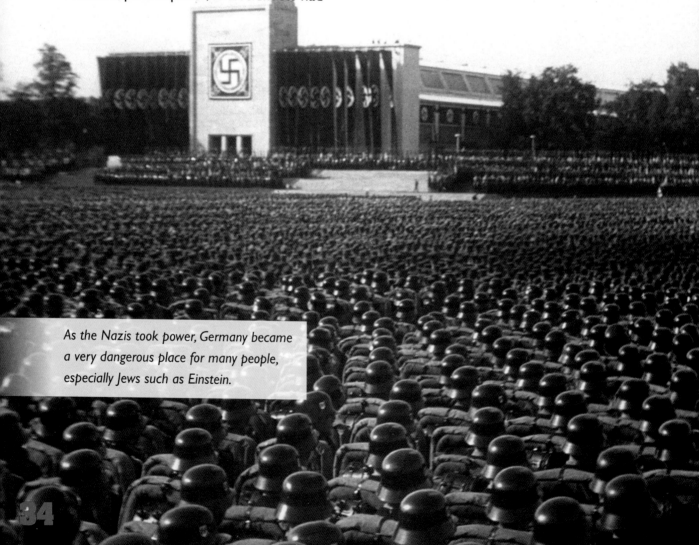

As the Nazis took power, Germany became a very dangerous place for many people, especially Jews such as Einstein.

Nazi Target

In Germany, Nazi scientists who supported Adolf Hitler dismissed Einstein's new relativity theory as "Jewish physics," and copies of his theories were burned. The Nazis organized special conferences to publically criticize his work. Some German physicists called for a "German physics," which meant studying only the discoveries and theories of non-Jews. In 1931, the Nazis published the book *One Hundred Authors Against Einstein*. In the book, scientists criticized Einstein's work and put forward reasons why Einstein was wrong. The book was really propaganda and another way of attacking the scientist.

IN THEIR OWN WORDS

Einstein said:

"The world is a dangerous place to live; not because of the people who are evil but because of the people who don't do anything about it."

Einstein in the United States

In 1933, the Nazi Party under Hitler came to power in Germany. Einstein immigrated to the United States and never returned to Germany. He was welcomed like a hero. Everybody wanted to meet the great man, from President Franklin D. Roosevelt to other brilliant scientists such as Edwin Hubble, the astronomer and discoverer of the Big Bang.

Einstein went to work at the Institute of Advanced Study in Princeton and took US citizenship. The Institute became the most famous research center in the world as other scientists left Europe to make new lives for themselves in the United States.

On October 1, 1940, Einstein became a US citizen.

IN THEIR OWN WORDS

Einstein said:

"A person who never made a mistake never tried anything new."

The Institute of Advanced Study was where Einstein worked in the United States. He worked there until his death.

Unfinished Business

Einstein retired from the Institute in 1945, but he continued to work on his theories. He hoped to find a single theory to join all his ideas about the universe together, but he did not succeed. This grand theory would explain everything that could happen in the universe. Many scientists thought that a single theory was not possible. A lot of theoretical research involves setting up ideas and testing them to see if they can be proven correct. There is a lot of trial and error. Decades later, no one has managed to figure out a theory to explain everything that can, does, and could happen in the universe.

Einstein with his wife, Elsa, are shown here.

The Manhattan Project and World War II

In 1939, the world once again found itself at war. World War II did not just divide nations; it signaled the start of the international arms race as countries tried to invent bigger and deadlier weapons.

Scientists in Hitler's Germany used Einstein's $E=mc^2$ to develop the atomic bomb. Horrified at this development and that he had helped in any way to make it happen, Einstein and other scientists wrote to the US president, Franklin D. Roosevelt. They urged him to carry out similar research in order to stop Hitler from having the upper hand in the war.

Between 1942 and 1946, the US government ran a top-secret research laboratory at Los Alamos in the New Mexico desert. There, the Manhattan Project involved an international team of physicists who were trying to build an atomic bomb. The physicists used the radioactive element plutonium to generate a gigantic amount of destructive energy.

Danish physicist Niels Bohr advanced quantum theory. He won the Nobel Prize in 1922, the year after Einstein won his Nobel Prize.

In 1945, the United States dropped two atomic bombs on Japan. Einstein was appalled that mankind had made something so terrible with the help of his scientific work.

Peace Campaigner

When the United States dropped atomic bombs on the Japanese cities of Hiroshima and Nagasaki in 1945, Einstein was horrified. Tens of thousands of people were killed in an instant. For the remainder of his life, Einstein devoted himself to peace and campaigning for an end to nuclear bombs. He feared that mankind would destroy itself with these weapons.

IN THEIR OWN WORDS

Einstein, horrified by nuclear weapons, said:

"I know not with what weapons World War III will be fought, but World War IV will be fought with sticks and stones."

CHAPTER 6
The Einstein Effect

On April 8, 1955, Albert Einstein died in Princeton, New Jersey. His death was front-page news around the world. Doctors preserved his brain for study to see if they could find out what made Einstein so smart. Arthur Eddington had passed away in 1944. He was considered the greatest astrophysicist of his age and continues to influence astronomers today.

Father of Modern Physics

Einstein's brilliance lives on today through the work of modern physicists. Scientists such as Professor Stephen Hawking are carrying on where Einstein left off. Hawking is building on and exploring Einstein's ideas about gravity and time and has also predicted that black holes give off radiation. Like Einstein, Hawking is world famous and has entered popular culture in cartoons, television comedies, and even the opening of the Olympic Games in London.

In 1927, the most brilliant physicists in the world met at the Solvay Institute in Belgium to discuss quantum theory. Marie Curie and Einstein are in the front row of this photo.

Stephen Hawking's books regularly top the best-seller charts. Einstein and Eddington paved the way for the modern interest in space by making the universe fascinating to everyone.

Eddington's Explorations

Arthur Eddington's influence has been felt in the worlds of physics, astrophysics, philosophy, and math. Perhaps most importantly, both Einstein and Eddington's work on black holes has led to modern-day physicists such as Roy Kerr and Leonard Susskind finding out even more about our universe.

BEHIND THE SCIENCE

Black holes are created when a gigantic star reaches the end of its life and explodes. We cannot see black holes, but we know they must exist because of their effect on objects near them such as stars and even whole galaxies. The gravitational pull of a black hole is so great that nothing can escape—not even light. If a satellite dish or a rocket were to fall into a black hole, they would be stretched apart by the power of the gravitational pull.

Einstein and Science Today

Far beneath the city of Geneva in Switzerland, 10,000 physicists from more than 60 countries are working to find out the meaning of matter. In a specially built circular tunnel called the Large Hadron Collider, scientists are trying to recreate the conditions that were present in the universe moments after the Big Bang.

Quantum physics (or quantum mechanics) is the study of tiny particles such as atoms and subatomic particles, which are tiny pieces of matter that are smaller than an atom. This branch of science has its origins in Einstein's great 1905 papers. The Large Hadron Collider is helping physicists to apply and test various theories about the universe. It is also helping them to discover even more than Einstein or Eddington dreamed of.

The Large Hadron Collider is the world's largest science experiment. Thousands of physicists are working there to discover what happened in the moments after the Big Bang took place.

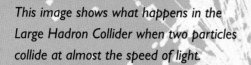
This image shows what happens in the Large Hadron Collider when two particles collide at almost the speed of light.

The Large Hadron Collider

The Large Hadron Collider was built to find out about all the particles, forces, and interactions that happen in the universe. Subatomic particles are sent around the tunnel at almost the speed of light. Every second, 600 million particle collisions occur which generate temperatures 100,000 hotter than the sun. Huge magnets collect the particles that are created by these collisions.

BEHIND THE SCIENCE

In the 1960s, the British physicist Peter Higgs suggested that other particles must exist that had not yet been discovered. He believed this was so because of the way particles behaved with each other. In March 2013, more than 40 years later, scientists at the Large Hadron Collider found evidence of the so-called Higgs-Boson particle.

Geniuses for All Time

In many ways, Albert Einstein and Arthur Eddington were an unlikely pair of scientists. They came from different countries, spoke different languages, and were on opposite sides when their countries were at war. However, their connection helped to change the path of science in the twentieth century and beyond.

Today, Einstein is considered by many to be the world's greatest scientist, while Eddington has been largely forgotten by the general public. Yet, without the quiet astronomer from Cambridge, it is possible that Einstein's work would never have made such an impact or reached such a wide audience, let alone be proven.

The universe is vast, and there are billions of galaxies left for scientists to explore.

Brilliant Minds

Both Einstein and Eddington have had a lasting effect on the way we see and think about the universe. Their work and discoveries shape our understanding about the space we inhabit. Their names are attached to dozens of important scientific theories, and such was their impact on wider society that their names can be found in the most unexpected places. There is an Eddington asteroid, and on the moon, there is the Eddington crater. Einstein, on the other hand, has streets, buildings, computers, telescopes, schools, and toys named after him. He also has an element named after him: einsteinium—a building block for life in honor of the man who changed the universe for us all.

33 USA

STAR TREK

1999

Even scriptwriters of the television show Star Trek drew upon Einstein and Eddington's theories! Who knows what exciting discovery scientists will make next or where they will take us...

IN THEIR OWN WORDS

Einstein said:

"Imagination is more important than knowledge. Knowledge is limited. Imagination encircles the world."

Glossary

anti-Semitic prejudice or discrimination against Jewish people

astronomer a person who studies the stars and planets

astrophysicist a person who studies the origin and development of stars, planets, and space

atom the smallest part of an element

black hole an area in space that is formed when stars collapse on themselves. Black holes have such a strong gravitational pull that no light or matter can escape

doctorate a post-graduate degree completed after a master's degree

electromagnetic spectrum a range of light in the universe

gravitational field the force of attraction between two or more objects with mass

immigrate to move to live in another country

mass the amount of matter an object contains

matter substance

molecule the smallest part of a chemical compound made up of one or more atoms

neutron a particle in the nucleus of an atom without any electric charge

nucleus the center of an atom that contains neutrons and protons

pacifist a person who does not believe in war

patent a document that gives the inventor the right to sell or make their invention

philosopher a person who tries to understand and explain the meaning of life and existence

photon the smallest quanta or particle of visible light

physicist a person who studies the substance, energy, and forces of matter

propaganda deliberately misleading publicity

quantum (plural is **quanta**) the smallest quantity of energy that exists in the universe

radiation energy given off from a source such as heat, light, or sound

radioactive describes the energy or particles emitted from unstable atoms such as uranium or plutonium. Radioactive materials can be harmful to human health

shunned deliberately ignored

subatomic any particle that is smaller than an atom, such as a proton

For More Information

Books

Berne, Jennifer. *On a Beam of Light: A Story of Albert Einstein*. San Francisco, CA: Chronicle Books, 2013.

Brake, Mark. *Really, Really Big Questions About Space And Time*. New York, NY: Kingfisher, 2010.

Venezia, Mike. *Albert Einstein Universal Genius* (Getting to Know the World's Greatest Inventors and Scientists). New York, NY: Scholastic Children's Press, 2008.

Websites

Fly through space and explore CERN's laboratory at:
www.cernland.net

Try out some of the interactive activities at NASA's kids site. Go to:
www.nasa.gov/audience/forkids/kidsclub/flash/

Learn more about the Higgs-Boson particle, the Big Bang, and all kinds of atomic particles at:
particleadventure.org

Index